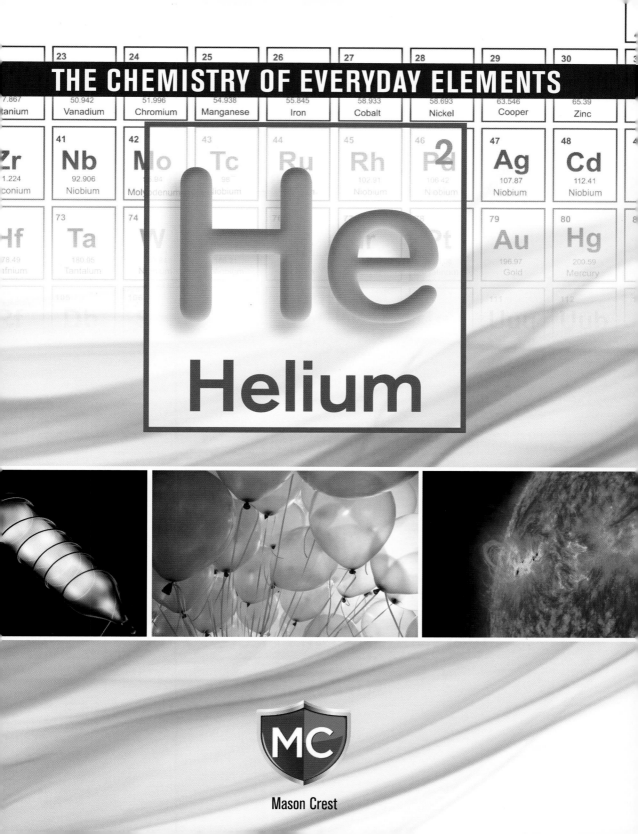

THE CHEMISTRY OF EVERYDAY ELEMENTS

He

2

Helium

Mason Crest

THE CHEMISTRY OF EVERYDAY ELEMENTS

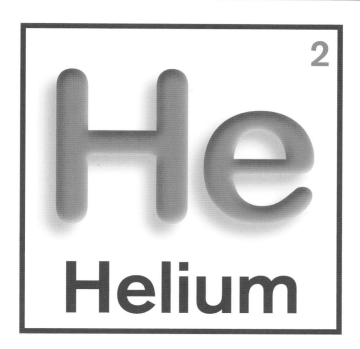

By Jane P. Gardner

Mason Crest
450 Parkway Drive, Suite D
Broomall, PA 19008
www.masoncrest.com

Series ISBN: 978-1-4222-3837-0
Hardback ISBN: 978-1-4222-3841-7
EBook ISBN: 978-1-4222-7946-5

First printing
1 3 5 7 9 8 6 4 2

Produced by Shoreline Publishing Group LLC
Santa Barbara, California
Editorial Director: James Buckley Jr.
Designer: Patty Kelley
www.shorelinepublishing.com

Library of Congress Cataloging-in-Publication Data on file with the Publisher.

Cover photographs by Dreamstime.com: Vangert (bkgd); Konstantin Sutyagin (balloons). NASA (sun).

QR Codes disclaimer:

He 2
Helium

KEY ICONS TO LOOK FOR

Words to Understand: These words with their easy-to-understand definitions will increase the reader's understanding of the text, while building vocabulary skills.

Sidebars: This boxed material within the main text allows readers to build knowledge, gain insights, explore possibilities, and broaden their perspectives by weaving together additional information to provide realistic and holistic perspectives.

Educational Videos: Readers can view videos by scanning our QR codes, providing them with additional educational content to supplement the text. Examples include news coverage, moments in history, speeches, iconic moments, and much more!

Text-Dependent Questions: These questions send the reader back to the text for more careful attention to the evidence presented here.

Research Projects: Readers are pointed toward areas of further inquiry connected to each chapter. Suggestions are provided for projects that encourage deeper research and analysis.

Series Glossary of Key Terms: This back-of-the-book glossary contains terminology used throughout this series. Words found here increase the reader's ability to read and comprehend higher-level books and articles in this field.

A Useful Gas

Look around you. What do you see? A book and, perhaps, a half-eaten blueberry muffin, sit on your desk. Outside your window, you might see clouds or rain or the sun shining, while you can feel your heart pump your blood throughout your body. All of those things—the solids, liquids, and gases around you—are composed of elements of the periodic table.

The periodic table is an arrangement of all the naturally occurring, and manufactured, elements known to humans. An element is a substance that cannot be broken down into other,

---

WORDS TO UNDERSTAND

isotope   an atom of a specific element that has a different number of neutrons; it has the same atomic number but a different atomic mass

---

separate, substances. There are 92 elements that can be found naturally on Earth and in space. The remaining 26 (and counting) have been manufactured and analyzed in a laboratory setting. These elements, alone or in combination with others, form and shape all the matter around us. From the air we breathe, to the water we drink, to the food we eat—all these things are made of elements.

We can learn a lot about an element just by finding its location on the periodic table. The periodic table is arranged into rows and columns by increasing atomic number. Each element has a unique atomic number. It is the number of protons in the nucleus of the atom. For example, helium has an atomic number of 2—there are two protons in the nucleus of an atom of helium. (All samples of an element have the same number of protons, but they may have a different number of neutrons in the nucleus. Atoms with the same number of protons but different number of neutrons are called **isotopes**.)

Each element on the periodic table is unique, having its own chemical and physical properties. Certain chemical properties can be interpreted based on which group or row an element is placed. The periodic table also gives important information such as the number of protons and neutrons in the nucleus of one atom of an element, the

He ²

Helium

number of electrons that surround the nucleus, the atomic mass, and the general size of the atom. The periodic table is a very useful tool as one begins to investigate chemistry and science in general. (For lots more on the periodic table, read *Understanding the Periodic Table*, another book in this series.)

This book is about the element helium. Helium, the second lightest element on the periodic table, has two protons and two neutrons in its nucleus. A stable atom of helium has two electrons. Helium is a gas under standard conditions.

How is helium a part of our lives? The most obvious are helium-filled balloons that float into the sky. Or maybe, you once sucked the air out of one of those balloons and amused your friends by sounding like Daffy Duck (though that is not really a safe practice). Those are the obvious uses, but helium is used for much more. As you will read, helium has applications in the world of medicine, high tech, and even in exploring space. While it is abundant in space, helium is found only in small quantities on Earth—in fact, it can sometimes be scarce. Because of this, helium is considered to be a nonrenewable resource and efforts are underway to conserve this element. The future of many things, including your party balloons, may depend on it.

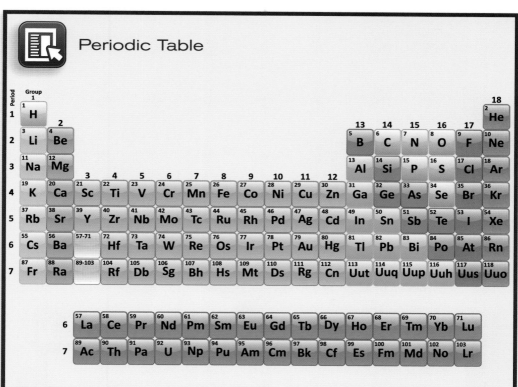

Periodic Table

Period	Group 1	2	3	4	5	6	7	8	9	10	11	12	13	14	15	16	17	18
1	1 H																	2 He
2	3 Li	4 Be											5 B	6 C	7 N	8 O	9 F	10 Ne
3	11 Na	12 Mg											13 Al	14 Si	15 P	16 S	17 Cl	18 Ar
4	19 K	20 Ca	21 Sc	22 Ti	23 V	24 Cr	25 Mn	26 Fe	27 Co	28 Ni	29 Cu	30 Zn	31 Ga	32 Ge	33 As	34 Se	35 Br	36 Kr
5	37 Rb	38 Sr	39 Y	40 Zr	41 Nb	42 Mo	43 Tc	44 Ru	45 Rh	46 Pd	47 Ag	48 Cd	49 In	50 Sn	51 Sb	52 Te	53 I	54 Xe
6	55 Cs	56 Ba	57-71	72 Hf	73 Ta	74 W	75 Re	76 Os	77 Ir	78 Pt	79 Au	80 Hg	81 Tl	82 Pb	83 Bi	84 Po	85 At	86 Rn
7	87 Fr	88 Ra	89-103	104 Rf	105 Db	106 Sg	107 Bh	108 Hs	109 Mt	110 Ds	111 Rg	112 Cn	113 Uut	114 Uuq	115 Uup	116 Uuh	117 Uus	118 Uuo

6	57 La	58 Ce	59 Pr	60 Nd	61 Pm	62 Sm	63 Eu	64 Gd	65 Tb	66 Dy	67 Ho	68 Er	69 Tm	70 Yb	71 Lu
7	89 Ac	90 Th	91 Pa	92 U	93 Np	94 Pu	95 Am	96 Cm	97 Bk	98 Cf	99 Es	100 Fm	101 Md	102 No	103 Lr

The Periodic Table of the Elements is arranged in numerical order. The number of each element is determined by the number of protons in its nucleus. The horizontal rows are called periods. The number of the elements increases across a period, from left to right. The vertical columns are called groups. Groups of elements share similar characteristics. The colors, which can vary depending on the way the creators design their version of the chart, also create related collections of elements, such as noble gases, metals, or nonmetals among others.

He ²

Helium

WORDS TO UNDERSTAND

inert   unable to bond with other matter

nanometer   one billionth of a meter

spectrum   the range of electromagnetic radiation
with respect to its wavelength or frequency; can
sometimes be observed by characteristic colors or light

wavelength   difference between two
corresponding parts of a wave

Discovery and History

Helium is the second most abundant element in the universe. Scientists estimate that 73 percent of the universe is hydrogen, 25 percent is helium, and the other 2 percent is made up of all the other elements. The same proportions of elements exist in our Sun as well. So it isn't much of a surprise that helium was discovered on the Sun in 1868. And yet, it wasn't discovered on Earth until the 1880s. Why did it take so long? For one reason, helium exists in Earth's atmosphere at very low levels. It is estimated that in Earth's atmosphere, only 1 out of every 200,000 particles is helium. It can be found in other places on Earth, too, but it turns out, people just weren't looking in the right places.

He 2
Helium

Spotting It in the Sun

In 1868, two astronomers were working independently on studying the spectral lines emitted by the Sun. Every element has a unique spectral line. In this way, they are similar to fingerprints. Each element displays its spectral line when the **wavelengths** of the elements are observed through a special filter or a spectrometer; this is much like visible light breaking into separate lines when passed through a prism.

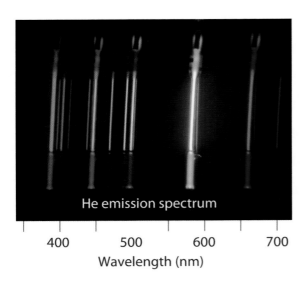

He emission spectrum

400   500   600   700
Wavelength (nm)

These colors represent the wavelengths of light passing through helium.

The French astronomer Pierre Janssen was working in India and looking at the **spectrum** of the light and energy emitted by the Sun during a solar eclipse. He observed a yellow spectral line with a wavelength of 587.49 **nanometers**—a wavelength that had not been seen before, in space or on Earth. He suspected he had found a new element in the solar radiation.

A few months later, the English astronomer Norman Lockyer was observing the spectral lines of solar radiation as it passed through the smog blanketing London. He found that same yellow spectral line and initially thought it might be a different isotope of hydrogen. But after extensive testing, he determined that it was indeed a new element.

Norman Lockyer

This was the first time that an element had been discovered in space before it was discovered on Earth. This newly discovered element was named after the Greek god of the Sun—Helios. It was assumed that the element was a metal and, since most metals have the suffix "-ium", it was named Helium. Helium, however, as the scientific community learned in the decades following its discovery, is not a metal.

Helium on Earth

Many in the scientific community were uncertain about this

He ²

Helium

discovery. Time passed, and helium was still not found on Earth. Some began to doubt the research that Janssen and Lockyer had done.

That all changed a few decades later in 1882, when the Italian physicist and meteorologist Luigi Palmieri was studying the historic eruptions of volcanoes in Italy. While studying the gases seeping from Mt. Vesuvius, he identified that same yellow spectral line—the line of the element named helium.

Then, in 1889, the American chemist William Hillebrand was experimenting with the mineral uraninite, which is composed of urani-

William Hillebrand

um and oxygen. He found that as uraninite dissolves in sulfuric acid, it releases an **inert** gas. He thought at the time that the inert gas was nitrogen, and while a portion of that gas was nitrogen, there was another gas involved.

Further research by the Scottish chemist William Ramsay proved that the inert gas from the dissolving uranium-rich mineral was in fact helium. Ramsay repeated Hillebrand's experiment using another mineral composed of ura-

The fiery heat from a volcano helped scientists locate more helium on Earth.

nium called clevite. He dissolved clevite samples in sulfuric acid and collected the gas. Spectral analysis of that inert gas confirmed that it was actually helium, the same element discovered on the Sun years before.

Uranium is an unstable element, which means that it will decay, or break down, over time. When an atom decays it releases energy. In the case of uranium, the energy it releases is in the form of an alpha particle. An alpha particle is composed of two protons and two neutrons—which is the nucleus of a helium atom! In other words, the radioactive decay of uranium releases helium.

He
Helium
2

 A New Discovery

In June 2016, a very significant deposit of helium was found in the continental crust beneath Tanzania, in the East African Rift Valley in east Africa. Scientists used a variety of methods to find this huge deposit, including techniques such creating images with seismographs. They believe that volcanic activity in the East African Rift Valley releases helium into the rock where it accumulated into a significant deposit. More exploration and investigation needs to be done at this site, but it looks as if this deposit could help alleviate the helium shortages the world has experienced in recent years.

Finding More Helium

Helium did exist on Earth after all, but the atoms of helium are so light that they are not held by Earth's gravity. Any helium that forms as a result of radioactive decay escapes into space.

Factories such as this one extract helium for commercial use.

Helium is, however, found in some reserves of natural gas. If captured from these natural gas fields, the helium can be used and distributed.

Finding helium on Earth was a significant discovery. It was first identified as a natural gas in 1903, when prospectors in the small town of Dexter, Kansas, had just located a reserve of natural gas that the town's citizens were hoping would bring prosperity and jobs. In recognition of this discovery, the town held a celebration. As a grand finale to the day, the plan was to release some of the natural gas and set it on fire with a hay bale. It was expected that the night sky would light up with a huge towering flame. However, when the burning hay bale was placed in the stream of natural gas, it went out. The organizers of

the event tried several more times to ignite the gas but were unable to.

A geology professor heard about the failed celebration. He traveled to Dexter, captured a sample of the gas, and sent it to a lab at the University of Kansas to be analyzed. Hamilton Cady and David

Natural gas burns off during extraction; helium comes from the same wells.

McFarland, two chemists from the university, tested the gas and found that it was 2 percent helium. This explained why it did not ignite. Hydrogen is a highly flammable gas, but helium does not burn. This was the first time that helium was confirmed to be associated with natural gas deposits. At the time it was not recognized how important this discovery could be economically, but that all changed as more and more uses for the inert gas were found.

Not all deposits of natural gas have accumulations of helium that can be collected. The geologic formations underground need to be very specifically organized. This is because, usually, the lighter-than-air helium will escape into the atmosphere as it is formed. Three conditions must be met for helium to accumulate in a deposit of natural gas:

1. There must be rocks that are rich in uranium and thorium (two radioactive elements).

2. Those rocks must have cracks and fractures to allow the helium to escape.

3. The porous rocks above them must be capped with a layer of rock through which the gas cannot pass.

If all these conditions are met, helium can accumulate.

He ²
Helium

This refinery produces both natural gas and helium . . . while it lasts.

Due to these very specific and strict conditions, there are only a few places in the world where it happens and from which helium can be captured. In the United States, natural gas fields in Texas, Colorado, Kansas, Oklahoma, Utah, and Wyoming produce a large portion of the world's helium resources. Around the world, the nations of Qatar, Algeria, Russia, and Canada are among the leaders in helium resources.

National Helium Reserve

Helium is a nonrenewable resource. That means although we can find new places where it has accumulated, we cannot produce more. It will eventually run out. The decay of uranium and similar elements—which produces helium—will slowly continue for the lifespan of Earth, but the helium that forms as a result of that process escapes into space. Capturing that helium for different uses is impractical. The helium associated with natural gas will only last as long as the reserves of natural gas. Many suggest that the world is facing a helium shortage—in the very near future.

The National Helium Reserve

This is actually not a new problem. In 1925, the government of the United States quickly became concerned about the uses of this newly discovered nonrenewable resource. The National Helium Reserve was established to strategically control the existing supplies of helium for use in transportation and national defense. This was a time of excess helium—more was being produced than was being used.

Helium

However, the need for helium changed over time. After World War II, the use of helium in airships and transportation declined, but new uses were found for the lighter-than-air gas, including applications for space travel, high technology, and in nuclear power plants and facilities that made nuclear weapons. Even with these new uses, the amount of helium that was being produced continued to exceed the amount being used.

Helium can be stored safely in these large metal cylinders.

In 1995, government scientists and Congress decided that the National Helium Reserve was not needed because the amount of helium had grown so much that "hoarding" it was not necessary. The US Congress started a program to sell helium and it was allowed to be sold at a great discount. Nearly half of the world's demand for helium was met with helium from the National Helium Reserve. This included helium being used both domestically and internationally. This much less expensive source of helium, sold from the Reserve, meant that the uses of helium were expanded to other applications. That is, applications that were typically dedicated to more expensive gases such as argon.

Nuclear power is one of the industries that use helium.

The sale of gas in the Reserve has proven to be a bit short-sighted. This once-large source of inexpensive helium has shrunk over time, of course, and prices have increased. However, demand continues to be high and it is estimated that the helium in the National Reserve will be depleted by 2021.

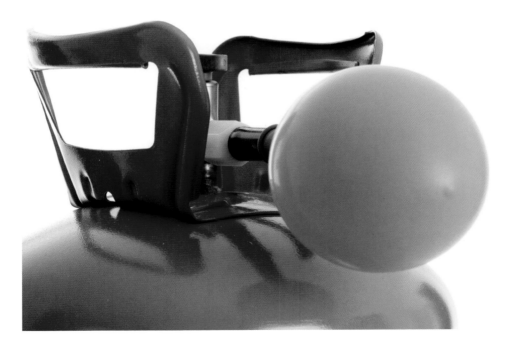

It's party time! Helium tanks fill balloons with the lighter-than-air gas.

The future of helium use relies on helium processing and recovery installations. Consumers around the world are waiting to see how this preserves the current need for the useful, and nonrenewable, resource.

 Text-Dependent Questions

1. About when was helium discovered on Earth?

2. Why is helium a nonrenewable resource?

3. Describe the National Helium Reserve.

Research Project

Read more about the process of extracting natural gas from the Earth. Make a pros and cons chart showing the positive and negative effects of natural gas.

He ²

Helium

WORDS TO UNDERSTAND

superfluid   matter that behaves as a fluid with no viscosity or resistance to flowing

viscosity   a property of a fluid that describes its resistance to flowing

Chemical Properties

Where did all the helium come from? How was it made? To start with, we need to look approximately 14 billion years ago—back to the Big Bang!

Immediately after the Big Bang, the universe was extremely hot and particles of matter were everywhere. As it began to cool, in the seconds that followed, particles such as protons, neutrons, and electrons formed. These became the basic building blocks for all that we know. In the first minutes after the Big Bang, atoms of hydrogen formed. A little after that three-minute mark, extra protons fused with some of the atoms of hydrogen, forming helium. Scientists believe that as this began to happen, about one helium atom was formed for every ten

Helium

hydrogen atoms—this is about the same ratio in which hydrogen and helium exist today.

The helium in the stars, for example the Sun, and in the universe as a whole, is the result of the Big Bang. However, as we learned in the previous chapter, the helium on Earth comes from a different source.

Helium as superfluid

It is believed that most of the helium on Earth is the result of radioactive decay. Some elements on the periodic table, such as uranium and thorium, are unstable. They continue to break down, or decay, and as a result release energy. Some of that energy released helium, which escapes Earth's gravity and moves into space.

The Superfluid

Helium is inert. That means that it doesn't react readily with other elements. But it has some interesting, unique characteristics. At certain temperatures, helium is a **superfluid**. Superfluids behave in such a way that they appear to defy gravity. This is because a superfluid has

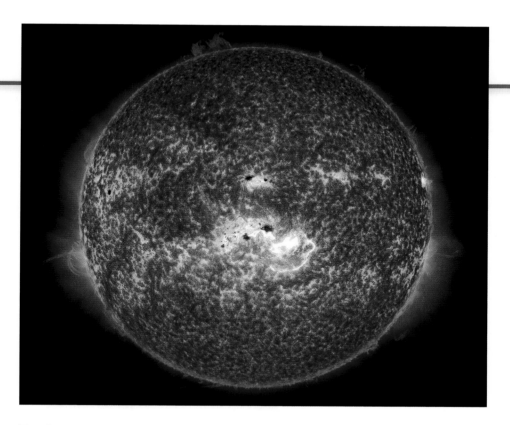

The Sun retains helium from its fiery birth billions of year ago.

no **viscosity**—the property of a fluid that describes its resistance to flowing; you might think of it as the "thickness" of the fluid. Helium, when cooled to just below its boiling point (-452°F/-269°C), becomes a superfluid. It is able to flow without being affected by friction or gravity. Helium has been seen seeping through microscopic cracks in a container, climbing up the side of its container, and staying still while its container is spun. Other materials behave like a superfluid under specific conditions; however, helium is one of the few substances where its superfluid behavior can be actually seen.

He ²

Helium

Helium "Rain" on Jupiter

From Earth, helium floats up and out of our atmosphere. On other planets in the Solar System however, the opposite is the case. Evidence gathered by scientists at the University of California, Berkeley, indicates that on Jupiter, helium seems to fall toward the planet's surface almost like rain. A close examination of the layers of Jupiter and its atmosphere shows that the outermost layer has very low concentrations of helium and neon. The innermost layers toward the interior of the planet are rich in helium and neon. Scientists interpret this to mean that the helium atoms condense and fall, like rain on Earth, dragging the neon atoms with it. It seems like a helium balloon on Jupiter would not be that much fun at all!

Helium is a nonrenewable resource because most of the helium produced by the radioactive decay of other elements escapes into space. Nonrenewable resources, such as coal, natural gas, and metal ores exist in finite supplies—once they are used up, there will be no more.

 Text-Dependent Questions

1. About how long ago was the Big Bang?

2. Name some ways that superfluids act.

3. What planet has helium "rain"?

Research Project

Find information on the Sun. What chemicals does it contain? What form do they take? Why is it so hot? Prepare a "Meet the Sun" chart listing its properties.

Helium and You

One of the most recognizable properties of helium is the way that it changes a person's voice when it is inhaled. Most of us have witnessed someone (if not tried it ourselves) untying a helium balloon and sucking in the helium gas that is inside. The result is a high, squeaky sound to your voice for a short period of time. A human's vocal cords vibrate and generate sound waves. The air we breathe on Earth is primarily nitrogen (78 percent) and the mass of nitrogen is much greater than the mass of helium. Nitrogen (and the air we breathe normally) is thus much denser, which means the sound waves your vocal cords generate will move more slowly through that air. When sound travels through the much less dense helium it moves much more quickly, resulting in the squeaky voice. In fact, at room temperature, sound travels through helium at 1,013 yards (927 m) per second, while it travels through normal air (nitrogen) at 376 yards (344 m) per second.

Many have questioned if it is healthy, or even safe, to take a deep breath of helium into your body. The National Inhalant Prevention Coalition says that inhaling helium can be dangerous, and in some cases even deadly. Inhaling helium can cut off the supply of oxygen to your cells. Gas bubbles of helium can enter your bloodstream, which is very dangerous. And, if the helium is inhaled directly from a pressurized tank, the lungs may rupture. While the number of deaths from inhaling helium is quite low, one has to ask if depriving your body of oxygen and perhaps causing permanent damage is worth the funny, squeaky voice a helium balloon can produce.

Helium and Health

Helium is unique in that it doesn't react with water or any other substance. These inert behaviors of helium mean that the gas is not toxic, does not generally harm the human body, and has no known adverse health effects. However, doctors and scientists have come up with several ways that helium can be used as a diagnostic tool, and even a treatment, for several common conditions and disorders.

Recently, doctors have been using helium to treat people with asthma. When patients, particularly children and teens, are admitted to the hospital with a severe asthma attack, the treatment needs to be quick and effective. Asthmatics suffer from constricted (narrowed) airways, as well as a buildup of mucus in the airways. The narrow airway and the thick mucus prevent a person from breathing in and out effectively, which in turn may trap air in the lungs. Doctors realized that the same property of helium that makes your voice sound high and squeaky

when you inhale it could help with the flow of air in and out of an asthmatic's lungs. Helium is lighter than the air we normally breathe, so the air that a person moves in and out of their lungs will move faster through helium. By giving a patient with asthma a dose of helium, the oxygen and carbon dioxide they are working to move in and out of their lungs will move more efficiently through the airways lined with helium.

Helium is given to asthma patients only in the most extreme cases, and always in the hospital. Overexposure to helium can be very dangerous, as it would displace the oxygen in the blood. While this is concerning, the greater concern for asthmatics is that they may be on a special type of therapy in which their bodies are given a higher concentration of oxygen to maintain a high level in their blood. Using a helium mixture to alleviate some of the symptoms of asthma could interfere with this mixture. Doctors, however, remain confident that with careful management and limited exposure, helium can be an effective treatment for extreme asthma attacks.

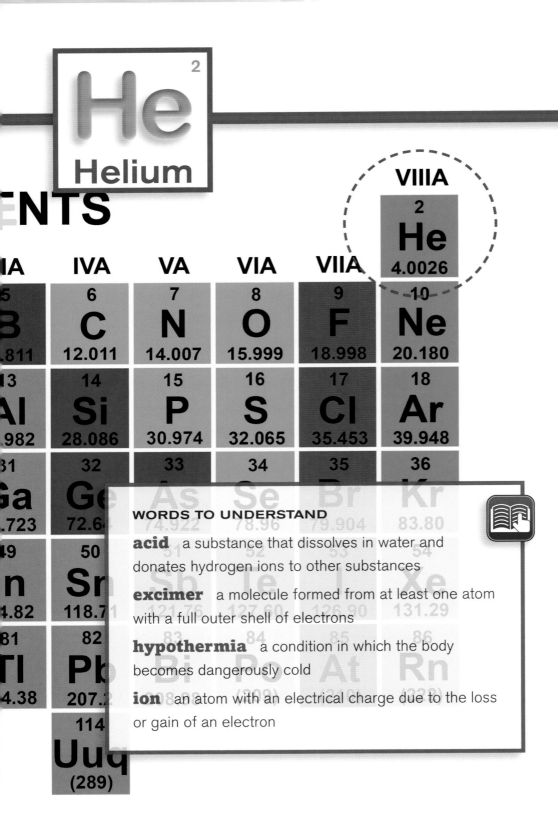

He
²

He

Helium

ENTS

VIIIA

2
He
4.0026

IA	IVA	VA	VIA	VIIA	
5	6	7	8	9	10
B	C	N	O	F	Ne
.811	12.011	14.007	15.999	18.998	20.180
13	14	15	16	17	18
Al	Si	P	S	Cl	Ar
.982	28.086	30.974	32.065	35.453	39.948
31	32	33	34	35	36
Ga	Ge	As	Se	Br	Kr
.723	72.64	74.922	78.96	79.904	83.80
49	50	51	52	53	54
In	Sn	Sb	Te	I	Xe
4.82	118.7	121.76	127.60	126.90	131.29
81	82	83	84	85	86
Tl	Pb	Bi	Po	At	Rn
4.38	207.2	(209)	(209)	(210)	(222)
	114				
	Uuq				
	(289)				

WORDS TO UNDERSTAND

acid a substance that dissolves in water and donates hydrogen ions to other substances

excimer a molecule formed from at least one atom with a full outer shell of electrons

hypothermia a condition in which the body becomes dangerously cold

ion an atom with an electrical charge due to the loss or gain of an electron

Helium Combines

Locate helium on the periodic table. Notice how it is on the far right hand column of the table? It is a member of Group 8A, the noble gases. Helium, along with neon, argon, krypton, xenon, and radium, are very stable. All atoms have electrons that circulate around the nucleus. The electrons are arranged in shells, or levels. Noble gases have the maximum number of electrons in their outermost shells. This is what makes them stable and unlikely to react with other atoms.

Helium is an inert noble gas. This means it does not easily combine with other elements. The noble gases were some of the last elements on the periodic table to be discovered. This is because they are so unreactive and are largely unlikely to form compounds with other elements. Noble gases are also

He ²

Helium

colorless and odorless, making them difficult to detect.

Some elements combine with others very readily. This process of combining involves either a sharing of electrons or a transfer of electrons. An atom will combine with another atom in order to fill the outermost layer with the maximum number of electrons. In the case of helium, the maximum number of electrons it can have in that outermost layer is two. As it already has two electrons there, there is no reason for helium to combine with another element.

However, it turns out that there is an exception to this. Helium can, in rare circumstances, form a unique compound with hydrogen. The compound that forms is called an **excimer**. An excimer is a very short-lived molecule that forms from at least one atom that has its outermost electron layer full. In

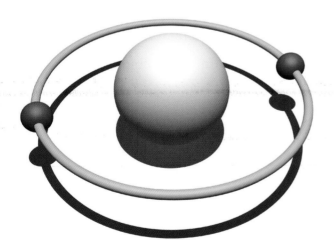

This diagram of a helium atom shows the two electrons that orbit its nucleus, giving the element its atomic number.

order for that one atom to react with another atom, there needs to be a lot of energy involved. The atom needs to be in a very excited state. It doesn't form very often. But it can give clues to one of the oldest questions there is —what was the origin of the universe like?

The Strange Case of Helium Hydride

The compound that helium forms is called helium hydride. Its chemical formula is HeH+. The only time that this compound is stable is when it is an **ion**—that is, the helium atom still only has two electrons but it is sharing one of those electrons with a hydrogen atom.

Interestingly, helium hydride is an **acid**. In fact, it is the strongest known acid. Helium hydride acid is much, much stronger than the common acids found in your home, such as lemon juice, vinegar, or soda. It is not found in a lab anywhere on Earth, but if it were, it would have some very significant industrial uses.

Helium hydride is thought to have been the first compound ever to exist anywhere in the universe. Consider this: for the first few minutes after the Big Bang, there was no matter. Nothing. The energy released during the Big Bang 13.7 billion years ago, was so intense that it took

He ²
Helium

a few minutes or so for the particles to cool down enough that ions could form. Hydrogen and its isotopes formed first, which paved the way for helium to form. Helium is believed to be the first element to form a bond, in this case, with a hydrogen ion. The evidence for this is difficult to pinpoint today but models used by scientists point to this unlikely compound forming early on in the history of the universe.

The Unique State of Helium

Helium may not combine under normal circumstances with other elements to form compounds, but in a way, it is because of helium that we have all the other elements on the periodic table. The carbon that makes up your body, the iron that is in your blood, the sodium that is part of the salt in your salt shaker—these elements were all made because of helium atoms in a distant star billions of years ago.

Consider how elements "grow" or are formed. Elements are defined by the number of protons in the nucleus. The number of neutrons and electrons in an atom of helium can vary; it is the fact that there are two protons in the nucleus that makes helium what it is. In order for a new element to form, protons need to be added to the nu-

Undersea Helium

Deep-sea divers often use a mixture of helium and oxygen called "heliox" in their tanks. It is used primarily for deep or very long dives. Recreational scuba divers don't typically use this

 mixture. Mixing helium with oxygen instead of nitrogen helps divers who have been under great pressures avoid a condition known as the "bends," or decompression sickness. The low density of helium makes breathing easier. But there are problems with using helium for this application. Helium conducts heat much better than nitrogen. This means that a person breathing a mixture of helium, rather than normal air, will lose body heat much faster than someone breathing air mixed with nitrogen. Losing body heat makes a diver more susceptible to **hypothermia**. Deep-sea divers often wear specially designed, insulated suits that are warmed with water pumped down from the surface. Before descending, they also might heat the heliox mixture they will breathe.

cleus. For example, the collision and resulting combination of three helium nuclei in a star billions of years ago produced an atom of carbon (carbon has 6 protons in the nucleus). When that star became a supernova, it exploded, hurling all of the elements that were made there into space. The carbon made from this, and other, massive stars eventually became the carbon that makes up all living things on Earth. While helium may not combine with other elements on Earth, it is

The gaseous cloud of a supernova spews out elements into deep space.

responsible for the other elements in the universe.

There is no good substitute for helium. Because of the unique properties of the element, even other noble gases aren't usually acceptable replacements for the element. Many of helium's applications require extremely cold conditions. Other elements would solidify at those temperatures. At times, argon can be substituted, especially in welding applications. Hydrogen would seem to be a likely substitute, but it is only possible when the explosive behavior of hydrogen is not an issue.

 Text-Dependent Questions

1. True or false: Helium is an inert noble gas.

2. Describe helium hydride.

3. In what activity do some people use "heliox"?

Research Project

Read more about supernovae. What are they made from? What causes them? Besides helium, what do they contribute to the universe?

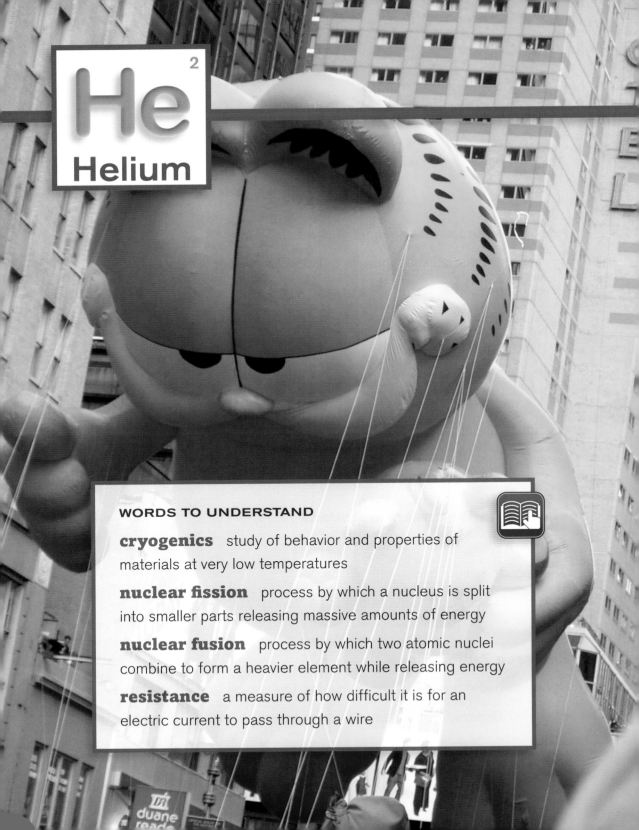

He
Helium

^{2}

WORDS TO UNDERSTAND

cryogenics   study of behavior and properties of materials at very low temperatures

nuclear fission   process by which a nucleus is split into smaller parts releasing massive amounts of energy

nuclear fusion   process by which two atomic nuclei combine to form a heavier element while releasing energy

resistance   a measure of how difficult it is for an electric current to pass through a wire

Helium in Our World

Watch the annual Macy's Thanksgiving Day parade in New York City and you will see many examples of how helium can be used in the amazing floats and balloons. But entertainment is not the only use for helium today. The fields of medicine, travel, space exploration, and technology rely heavily on this inert, lighter-than-air gas.

Medicine

The magnetic resonance imaging machine (MRI) used to peer inside the human body is cooled by liquid helium. An MRI machine uses superconducting magnets to produce a scan and an image of the body. Electricity passes through the coils of

wire in the magnet, producing a tremendous amount of energy. In order for this to happen, the **resistance** in the wire must be very close to zero. This can only be accomplished at very low temperatures, which calls for the use of liquid helium at -452.4 °F (-269.1°C). Liquid helium is the only known substance that can safely reach this temperature in such a setting.

Parade!

More than 300,000 cubic feet of helium are used to inflate the giant balloons featured in the Macy's Thanksgiving Day Parade. That is about the same volume as over two million gallons of milk! After the parade, the helium is released back into the atmosphere.

For years, the scanning electron microscope (SEM) has been used as a fundamental tool in the imaging of biological samples. The SEM uses electrons, rather than light, to form an image. The information ob-

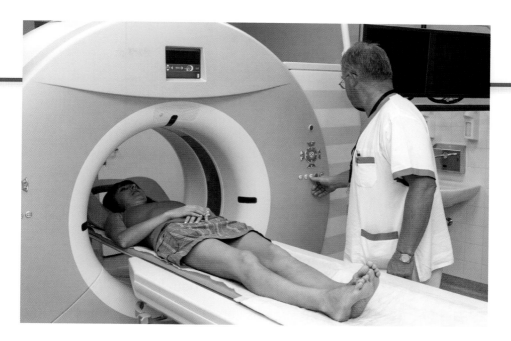

The cooling power of helium makes body-scanning MRI machines possible.

tained from and advances made with the SEM are indisputable, but its use is not without limitations. The SEM does not do well at very high resolutions and the images can be hampered by the properties of a soft material, such as a biological sample. An alternative has been developed—the helium ion microscope (HIM). The resolution with this type of microscope is much greater, and it is possible to see deeper into the biological sample with the scan. The technology uses a beam of helium ions that can cut a sample to less than a nanometer of resolution. While the resolution is better than the SEM and little damage is done to the sample being analyzed with the HIM, this new technology is significantly more expensive than the SEM. But without helium, it would be impossible!

A Lifting Gas

Helium balloons float because the gas is literally "lighter than air." That is, it is lighter than the air we breathe close to Earth's surface. Lighter-than-air hydrogen and helium have both historically been used as a lifting gas to fill aircraft such as zeppelins, dirigibles, and blimps.

Hydrogen is the lightest element in the universe. It can be produced easily and inexpensively. But it is highly flammable and therefore quite dangerous. Airships fueled by hydrogen can explode, as the German zeppelin *Hindenburg* did so famously in 1938. Because of this, no US airship has used hydrogen since the US Army airship *Roma* crashed in a fiery explosion in 1922. Thirty-four people lost their lives in that disaster and since then the US military has inflated airships with helium.

The deadly explosion of the *Hindenburg* spelled the end of hydrogen aircraft.

Today, inventors are trying new aircraft that would be filled with helium.

Helium is a good choice as a lifting gas. It is not flammable, and it is the second lightest element on Earth. While it is twice as heavy as hydrogen, if pure helium is used, it can provide 90 percent of the lifting power of hydrogen. Helium is more expensive, and is not as readily available. Today, smaller craft, such as weather balloons, are still filled with helium. Helium is not used on such a wide scale anymore for these sorts of vehicles due to its cost and increasing scarcity.

It looks as if the helium aircraft might be making a comeback, at least in a few instances. In the past few years, engineers and scientists have designed several experimental craft that use helium and its lighter-than-air properties. A helium-filled airplane constructed in the UK has a unique design. It is made of very light carbon fiber and has a bulbous shape with a helium-filled central area. The combination of these two factors makes the airplane very light and able to take off and land at lower speeds than other airplanes. As a result, the runways

that it can use can be much shorter—making the plane useful in disaster zones and other remote locations.

A company in California is working on developing a helium-filled zeppelin that could land and take off vertically. The idea is to use a very buoyant gas, such as helium, to control this movement. Other

This zeppelin in California aims to become a cargo-carrying helium airship.

fuels or the cargo that the craft would carry would help act as a ballast to control the movement of the ship. There are designs for this type of airship, but the price of the helium gas can sometimes make the use of them costly.

Technology

Today's technology is being shaped, and cooled, by helium. In fact, a company has developed a computer hard drive that is sealed and operates in an environment composed of helium. Helium is significantly less dense than the air around us. As a result, a hard drive operating within a helium environment will use less power, create less heat, and be less noisy. The benefit of all this is a higher storage capacity on the hard drive and a lower cost of operation. The less dense helium environment allows the hard drive to spin much faster, with less resistance. This reduction in resistance and friction results in a lower temperature. Sometimes your cell phone or your laptop computer becomes warm, or even hot, to the touch during use. The hard drive operating in the helium environment on average runs at 39.2°F (4°C) lower than normal. This saves power as well. Sealing a hard

Helium 2

drive within a helium environment is quite expensive, but because of the increase in storage capacity and the decreases in operating costs, the saving are realized quite quickly.

Science

The true origins of the universe are not well understood. Scientists have a working hypothesis of the events that surrounded the Big Bang, but they have yet to determine exactly what happened before and after this event. Between 1998 and 2008, more than 10,000 scientists and engineers designed and built the Large Hadron Collider (LHC) in a tunnel on the border between France and Switzerland. It is the largest machine and the largest particle collider in the world. The LHC was designed to let scientists test their predictions about high energy physics and the origins of the universe.

The LHC uses more than 1,600 superconducting magnets. These together weigh more than 27 tons! Helium must be used to keep those

How the LHC works.

magnets at a temperature of 1.9 Kelvin (or about -217 °C/-362.2°F). Specifically, about 96 tons of an isotope of helium—the superfluid helium-4—needs to be used. The use of this much liquid helium makes the LHC the largest **cryogenic** facility operating at these temperatures anywhere in the world.

Leak Detection

Helium has other, less technical, uses as well. Due to the very small size of a helium atom, helium is able to escape through very small cracks and holes. Helium gas is used to detect leaks in fuel systems or systems under very high vacuum. Also, helium doesn't react with metals. Welders often protect their metals from rust and other processes by welding within a helium-rich environment.

He ²
Helium

Space Travel

NASA uses liquid hydrogen as a propellant for its rockets and spacecraft. And yet, NASA uses up to 100 million cubic feet of helium each year. Helium is the only gas that can purge, or clean out, the hydrogen lines that supply the launch pads. Hydrogen is very light, which makes it a great choice for space travel. It also burns very explosively, reaching temperatures of 5,500°F (3,037°C). Hydrogen is cryogenic—

The explosive power of liquid hydrogen has made visits to distant planets possible.

Supercooling helium has helped scientists date ancient artifacts.

it can only be liquefied at very, very low temperatures. It must be stored at -423°F (-253°C). As a result, as NASA pipes the liquid hydrogen to the launch pads, any hydrogen that is left in the lines will turn to a gas very quickly . . . and hydrogen gas is extremely flammable. Other gases, such as oxygen and nitrogen, will turn solid at the cryogenic temperatures that are in the lines. Helium is the only element that turns to a liquid at temperatures lower than that of hydrogen. That means helium gas can be used to clean out the lines, preventing a potentially explosive reaction with the leftover hydrogen.

Helium Dating

There are eight identified isotopes of helium (remember, an isotope is a version of an element). The majority of the helium on Earth is in the form of helium-4. A very small percentage is helium-3, and

the other six isotopes are very rare. Helium-3 has a very specific use for scientists trying to find out how old something is. When a radio-active, or parent isotope of an element decays, it continues to do so until it becomes a stable "daughter" isotope. Scientists can measure the proportions of the original element and its stable daughter to de-termine the age of a substance. That is, they can see how much has changed and calculate how long that took to change. For example, tritium is a radioactive isotope of hydrogen. It decays to become the stable daughter isotope of helium-3. This process does not take that long—just over 12 years for half of the atoms of tritium to decay into stable helium-3. As a result, this method of measuring the amount of tritium and helium-3 in a sample can be used to determine the age of different substances. Currently, its most significant use is in determin-ing the age of a sample of groundwater.

Everyday Uses

Have you ever looked closely at the device used in a supermarket or other store to scan the UPC symbol on an item? Many times it lets off a red beam of light as the item is passed over it. In most cases, this

Helium helps control the laser light used in scanners like this one.

scanner uses a mixture of helium and neon gases. An electric current is passed through a tube containing the gas mixture, which produces light in the form of a laser. In most cases, the mixture is 10 parts helium to 1 part neon. This type of laser is inexpensive, which make it a good choice for stores and supermarkets looking to use this technology for keeping records, restocking, and checkout counters. The beam that is emitted by the laser is strong enough to read bar codes and UPC labels, but weak enough to not damage the eyes of someone who may look at it.

A Source of Energy?

As the world looks to the future, and different sources of energy, the focus for many has turned to nuclear power. At the moment, most

of the existing nuclear power plants rely on **nuclear fission**. Nucle-ar fission is a process by which nuclei of certain atoms, such as urani-um, are split apart. This releases energy that can then be harnessed. Unfortunately, it also releases radioactivity and other by-products

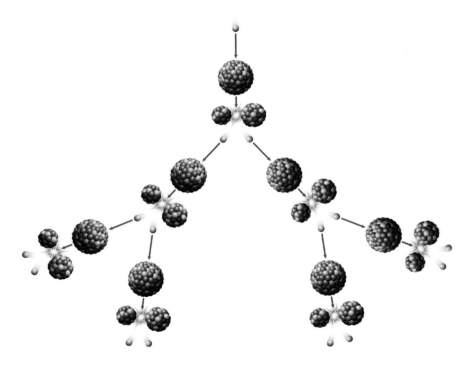

This diagram shows the chain reaction (start at the top) in nuclear fission.

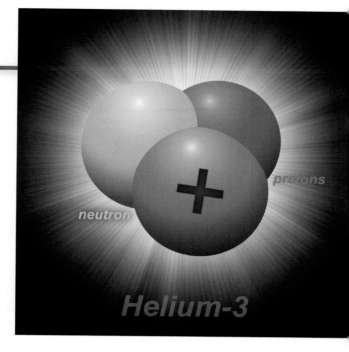

neutron

protons

Helium-3

Can this isotope of helium be a future power source? Scientists are looking at this rare substance carefully.

that are dangerous and need to be stored in specialized containers for centuries.

Scientists have been looking to create nuclear power through the process of **nuclear fusion**. They have been experimenting with using an isotope of helium, helium-3, and an isotope of hydrogen as the fuel to produce atomic energy.

Helium-3 has been shown to be a very effective fuel in this process, responsible for creating a tremendous amount of energy with basically no waste products or radiation. The problem is that the supply of helium-3 on Earth is very, very limited, so scientists have started to look elsewhere for a source of this helium isotope. And the first place they're looking is . . . the Moon.

Helium-3 is found within the solar winds that come from the Sun. Earth's atmosphere serves as a protective barrier, blocking out most

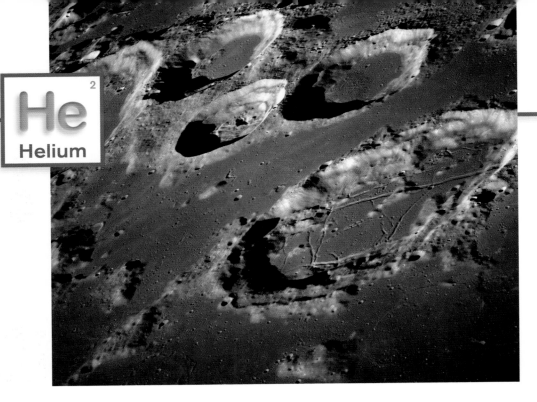

The surface of the Moon, which might contain a huge supply of helium-3.

of the solar wind and therefore a supply of He-3. The Moon, however, with its very thin and irregular atmosphere, does not keep out the solar wind. He-3 has been bombarding the surface of the Moon for nearly 5 billion years and has been absorbed by the soil there. Estimates put the amount of helium-3 in the lunar soil to be about 1,100,000 metric tons!

Scientists in favor of mining the lunar surface for helium-3 and using it for fusion have calculated that about 25 tons of helium-3 could provide enough power for the entire United States for one year. In other words with all the other mineral deposits on the Moon that we have thought about harvesting, helium-3 would be the most economical.

The United States, Russia and China are all working on methods to collect, and bring back to Earth, this potentially valuable resource.

Helium is not the most famous element, nor is it the most useful or important one for our health. But it has properties that scientists are continuing to explore in an effort to make our lives on Earth better. So next time you see party balloons, don't think of making funny voices . . . think about how the rare gas that makes those balloons float might one day help power your car or save your life.

 Text-Dependent Questions

1. Why can using helium improve computer hard drives?

2. Name the German hydrogen zeppellin that exploded.

3. How does helium help people working in retail stores?

Research Project

Read more about the shortage of helium on Earth. Find three things that people or governments are doing to conserve this important element.

He
2
Helium

FIND OUT MORE

Books

Fernandes, Bonnie Juettner. *The Large Hadron Collider*. Chicago: Norwood House Press, 2013.

Gray, Theodore. *Elements: A Visual Exploration of Every Known Atom in the Universe*. New York: Black Dog & Leventhal, 2012.

Nath, Biman B. *The Story of Helium and the Birth of Astrophysics*. New York, NY: Springer, 2013.

Websites

http://imagine.gsfc.nasa.gov/science/toolbox/spectra1.html
NASA has an interactive website that reviews atomic spectra.

www.newscientist.com/article/dn24571-helium-filled-airplane-could-help-in-disaster-zones/
Find out more about a potential use of helium aircrafts in this article.

www.popularmechanics.com/science/health/a4046/why-is-there-a-helium-shortage-10031229/
Is there really a helium crisis on Earth? Read on to find out more.

SERIES GLOSSARY OF KEY TERMS

carbohydrates a group of organic compounds including sugars, starches, and fiber

conductivity the ability of a substance for heat or electricity to pass through it

inert unable to bond with other matter

ion an atom with an electrical charge due to the loss or gain of an electron

isotope an atom of a specific element that has a different number of neutrons; it has the same atomic number but a different mass

nuclear fission process by which a nucleus is split into smaller parts releasing massive amounts of energy

nuclear fusion process by which two atomic nuclei combine to form a heavier element while releasing energy

organic compound a chemical compound in which one or more atoms of carbon are linked to atoms of other elements (most commonly hydrogen, oxygen, or nitrogen)

spectrum the range of electromagnetic radiation with respect to its wavelength or frequency; can sometimes be observed by characteristic colors or light

solubility the ability of a substance to dissolve in a liquid

He ²
Helium

INDEX

Photo Credits

Dreamstime.com: Konstantin Sutyagin 10, Satori13 15, industrytravel 16, Rudmer Zwerver 17, Worldshots 18, Uko Jesita 23, Rmarmion 24, William Attard McCarthy 26, Piksel 32, Aleg Baranau 34, Laschi 36, Bobyramone 38, Simon Gurney 41, Sam20140218 44, Marcelahirkova 46, Marian Vejcik 47, Taina Sohlman 49, Terry Mapstone 52, Flora Paul Daniel 55, Ultraone 57, Peter Hermes Furian 58. Penn State University: 12; Wellcome/Walery/Wikimedia 13; RasGas 20; Leo Koivulehto/Wikimedia 22; NASA 29, 30, 42, 54, 60; US Navy: 48; Airlander 50; Brookhaven National Laboratory 59.

About the Author

Jane P. Gardner has written more than 30 books for young and young-adult readers on science and other topics. She authored the *Science 24/7* series as well as several titles in the *Black Achievement in Science* series. In addition to her writing career, she also has years of classroom teaching experience. Jane taught middle school and high school science and currently teaches Chemistry at North Shore Community College in Massachusetts. She lives in eastern Massachusetts with her husband and two sons.